Strategic Studies Institute Monograph

THE STRATEGIC LOGIC OF THE
CONTEMPORARY SECURITY DILEMMA

Max G. Manwaring

I0447274

December 2011

FOREWORD

This monograph stems from the tactical and operational frustrations of the U.S. Southern Command (USSOUTHCOM) regarding citizen and collective security in the Western Hemisphere. These frustrations have been demonstrated in each of the annual colloquia that the Strategic Studies Institute and its partners, Florida International University, the National Defense University, and USSOUTHCOM have conducted over the past 8 years. This monograph also reflects similar frustrations expressed by other U.S. Government organizations and agencies, as well as by various hemispheric governments and security institutions.

The urgency and importance of the security issue have generated four related themes. First, several countries in Latin America are paradigms of the failing state and have enormous implications for the stability, development, democracy, prosperity, and peace of the entire Western Hemisphere. Second, the transnational drug and arms trafficking, paramilitary, insurgent, and gang organizations in Mexico, Central and South America, and the Caribbean Basin are perpetrating a level of corruption, criminality, human horror, and internal instability that—if left unchecked at the strategic level—can ultimately threaten the collapse of various states and undermine the security and sovereignty of neighbors. Third, poverty, social exclusion, environmental degradation, and political-economic-social expectations—and the conflicts generated by these indirect and implicit threats to stability and human well-being—lead to further degeneration of citizen security. Fourth, these threats constitute a serious challenge to U.S. national security, well-being, and position in the global community. Unfortunately, a strategic-level debate has largely been absent from all this discourse.

The reality and severity of the threats associated with transnational security issues indicate that the United States and its national and international partners need a new paradigm for the conduct of contemporary warfare and an accompanying new paradigm for strategic leader development. The strategic-level basis of these new paradigms can be found in the fact that the global community is redefining security in terms of nothing less than a reconceptualization of sovereignty. In the past, sovereignty was the acknowledged and/or real control of territory and the people in it. Now, sovereignty is the responsibility of governments to protect the well-being of their peoples and to prevent great harm to those peoples. The security dilemma has now become: Why, when, and how to intervene to protect people and prevent egregious human suffering? Thus, we address some of the strategic-level questions and recommendations that arise from this elaboration. We will probably generate more questions than answers, but it is time to begin the strategic-level discussion.

This monograph comes at a critical juncture—a time of promise for globalization, creating a world that has become increasingly interconnected and a positive force for good government, human rights, the environment, peace, and prosperity. At the same time, there is profound concern that the fragmentation associated with globalization is acting as a negative force—leading people everywhere to seek refuge in smaller groups, characterized by isolationism, separatism, fanaticism, and deteriorating citizen security and well-being. The Strategic Studies Institute is pleased to offer this monograph as part of a continuing effort to inform the security debate, move it to a higher level, and support the best interests of the governments and peoples of the Western Hemisphere and the rest of the world.

DOUGLAS C. LOVELACE, JR.
Director
Strategic Studies Institute

ABOUT THE AUTHOR

MAX G. MANWARING is a Professor of Military Strategy in the Strategic Studies Institute (SSI) of the U.S. Army War College (USAWC), has held the General Douglas MacArthur Chair of Research at the USAWC, and is a retired U.S. Army colonel. He has served in various civilian and military positions, including the U.S. Southern Command (USSOUTHCOM), the Defense Intelligence Agency, Dickinson College, and Memphis University. Dr. Manwaring is the author and co-author of several articles, chapters, and books dealing with Latin American security affairs, political-military affairs, and insurgency and counter-insurgency. His most recent book is *The Complexity of Modern Irregular War* (Norman, OK: University of Oklahoma Press, forthcoming). His most recent article is "Three Lessons from Contemporary Challenges to Security," in *PRISM*, Vol. 2, No. 3 (June 2011). His most recent SSI monograph is *The Strategic Logic of the Contemporary Security Dilemma* (Carlisle, PA: Strategic Studies Institute, U.S. Army War College, forthcoming). Dr. Manwaring is a graduate of the U.S. Army War College, and holds an M.A. and a Ph.D. in political science from the University of Illinois.

SUMMARY

From the Peace of Westphalia in 1648 to the end
of World War II and beyond the Cold War period,
the prevailing assumption was that interstate warfare
would continue to be the dominant threat to global
peace and prosperity. Today's wars, by contrast, are
intrastate conflicts that take place mainly within — not
across — national borders. As a consequence, the disease of intrastate conflict has been allowed to rage relatively unchecked across large areas of the world, and
has devastated the lives of millions of human beings.
At the same time, indirect and implicit unmet needs
(e.g., poverty) lead people into greater and greater
personal and collective insecurity.

In the past, the traditional security dilemma was:
What is defensive, and what is aggressive? This problem has never been sorted out. It depends entirely on
one's interpretation — based on culture, values, external relationships, interests, and concepts of threat
to national security. As one contemporary example,
China considers the development of a large, modern
navy as defensive. Given the interests and vulnerabilities of Japan, that country considers China's efforts to
be offensive — and potentially aggressive. Clearly, the
security dilemma of the past retains a certain validity.
Nevertheless, contemporary realities have given rise
to a new, broad, complicated, and more ambiguous
security dilemma. Thus, two new types of threats have
been introduced into the contemporary global security arena: 1) hegemonic nonstate actors (e.g., insurgents, transnational criminal organizations, terrorists,
private armies, and gangs), which are taking on roles
that were once reserved exclusively for traditional
nation-states; and, 2) indirect and implicit threats to

stability and human well-being (e.g., poverty; social exclusion; environmental degradation; and political, economic, and social expectations).

This monograph provides a brief examination of: 1) the relatively recent evolution of international conventions and declarations that contribute directly to the contemporary diplomatic-legal definition of security; 2) salient scholarly thinking relating to political-diplomatic-legal principles that have become integral parts of the United Nations (and various other international efforts to confront threats to citizen and collective security and human well-being); and, 3) selected post-Cold War military responses to hegemonic non-state actors. The security dilemma, then, is more than a question of determining what aggression is and what aggression is not. Rather, it is now a question of: Why, when, and how to intervene to protect people and prevent egregious human suffering. This question, in turn, encompasses more than a redefinition of security. It is nothing less than a redefinition of sovereignty. Sovereignty was, in the past, the control of territory and the people in it. Sovereignty is now the responsibility to protect peoples' well-being in a given territory.

Accordingly, we must adapt our approach to security and organize our institutions to address the concept of unconventional intrastate war (e.g., Fourth Generation War), and the overwhelming reality that, just as the world has evolved from an industrial society to an information-based society, so has warfare. The reality of this evolution demonstrates the need for a new paradigm of conflict based on the fact that information—not firepower—is the currency upon which war is now conducted. The new primary center of gravity is public opinion and political leadership.

The "new" instruments of power are intelligence, public diplomacy, media, time, and flexibility.

The next and probably most important effort in the process of developing a new strategic-level paradigm for conflict is educational (cognitive). The effort must be directed at civilian and military leaders to help them understand and use appropriate combinations of national and international power in institutionalizing a shift in the contemporary strategic leadership development paradigm. In the context of new paradigms of conflict and leader development, we will address conceptual and organizational questions and recommendations that arise out of that elaboration. In Clausewitzian terms, all these questions and recommendations are designed to help decisionmakers, policymakers, opinion makers, and operators understand precisely the kind of conflict they are thinking about, what it is not, and what they must understand to conduct it successfully.

THE STRATEGIC LOGIC OF THE CONTEMPORARY SECURITY DILEMMA

In 1996, Boutros-Boutros Ghali, the Secretary General of the United Nations (UN), described the most important dialectics at work in the post-Cold War world as globalization and fragmentation. He observed that globalization was creating a world that has become increasingly interconnected, and a positive force for, *inter alia*, decolonization, good government, development, human rights, and the environment. The Secretary General understood, too, that fragmentation was acting as a negative force—leading people everywhere to seek refuge in smaller groups, characterized by isolationism, separatism, fanaticism, and the proliferation of intrastate conflict. He also recognized that fragmentation can act as a major cause—related to poverty, social exclusion, and poor governance—of state failure. Fragmentation, in turn, exposes the global community to increased human migration, the proliferation of nonstate actors (good and bad), and transnational criminal activity. At the same time, indirect and implicit unmet needs (e.g., poverty) lead people into greater and greater personal and collective insecurity. Thus, two new types of threats have been introduced into the global security arena. They are: 1) hegemonic nonstate actors (e.g., insurgents, transnational criminal organizations, terrorists, private armies, and gangs) that are taking on roles once reserved exclusively for traditional nation-states; and, 2) indirect and implicit threats to stability and human well-being (e.g., poverty; social exclusion; environmental degradation; and political, economic, and social expectations).[1]

1

Up to the end of World War II, and into and after the Cold War period, the prevailing assumption was that interstate warfare was and would continue to be the dominant threat to global peace. Today's wars, by contrast, are intrastate conflicts that take place mainly within—not across—national borders. As a consequence, "The disease of [intrastate] conflict has been allowed to rage relatively unchecked across large areas of the world, and has devastated the lives of millions of human beings."[2] It is within this dialectical context that the security dilemma concept has broadened from the traditional notion of defense against nation-state military aggression to that of complex and ambiguous intrastate conflict and indirect internal security issues the world is experiencing in the 21st century. This monograph examines **The Security Dilemma: Past and Present.** Then, it discusses at some length **The Development of the Contemporary Security Dilemma Concept** as analyzed by international organizations, key scholars, and some practitioners. Third, it addresses some of the **Questions and Recommendations that Arise** out of that elaboration, followed by a brief **Conclusion.**

The primary intent of this think piece is to examine some important aspects of contemporary and future asymmetric irregular warfare and internal security implications. From this vantage point, anyone who has the responsibility of dealing with, analyzing, planning, implementing, and/or reporting on collective and personal citizen security threats might generate successes and might turn those successes into strategic victories.

THE SECURITY DILEMMA: PAST AND PRESENT

International Relations texts teach that the anarchy of a century of religious wars and the Thirty Years War generated a determination on the part of the controlling elites of 17th-century Europe to devise an interstate system of mutual respect and forbearance. The European nations hoped that such an agreement might prevent the senseless carnage of the past from happening again. The result of these efforts—which took place over a period of 4 years—was the Peace of Westphalia. In the various documents that were signed in 1648, the European monarchs of the day pledged to honor each other's sovereignty over the territory and people affirmed to be theirs. That sovereignty was considered to be sacrosanct. Intervention by one state into the domestic affairs of another nation-state (including vital mercantilist interests abroad) was defined as aggression. From 1648 to the present, the Westphalian system addressed the sovereignty of nation-states only; the system was military-economic, and primarily defensive.[3]

More recently, classical realist scholar Hans Morgenthau wrote about imperial (hegemonic) state powers operating outside the international (Westphalian) structure, with the objective of overthrowing an existing system and replacing it with something else. Nazi Germany under Adolph Hitler was a case in point.[4] Later, Robert Gilpin discussed how uneven growth in military, economic, and technological power over time might convince a relatively weaker power that the benefits of attempting to change something in the existing international order could outweigh the risks. In that context, Albert Camus reminds us that Hitler's attempt to change the international system began as a gang (the Brown Shirts) effort in Munich, Germany. Over the period 1933-45, Hitler imposed the ethics of a criminal gang on an entire civilization.[5] Nevertheless, grand-scale theories on violently and radically changing a given political-economic-social system, such as those of Morganthau, Gilpin, and others, still apply only to nation-states.[6] The mainstream international relations literature does not take violent nonstate groups seriously, and generally teaches that hegemonic nonstate actors are basically local law enforcement problems that do not require sustained national security policy attention.[7]

A notable but not well-known exception to this position was expressed by Kimbra L. Fishel after the proverbial wake-up call on September 11, 2001 (9/11). Fishel pointed out several realities relevant to the contemporary global security system. First, she indicated that al Qaeda had succeeded in doing what no other terrorist organization had accomplished: elevating asymmetric, insurgent warfare onto the global arena. She also noted that al Qaeda and its leadership do not pretend to reform an unjust order or redress perceived grievances.[8] Their aim is radical and total change—that is, the intent is to destroy perceived Western and regional enemies and replace them as the predominant global powers.[9] Additionally, Fishel pointed out that:

- Some nonstate actors (insurgents, private armies, terrorists, transnational criminal organizations, and gangs) are, in fact, engaged in hegemonic war (conflict), as if they were nation-states attempting to overthrow or control one another;
- Terrorism, rather than conventional weaponry, is a very practical, calculated, cynical, and in-

4

expensive tactic or strategy for the weak to use against the strong;

- Many violent nonstate actors have institutionalized political-psychological innovations and exploited poverty and other indirect issues as substitutes for expensive, highly technical conventional weapons systems;
- The ends of contemporary intrastate conflict are changing from the absolute objectives of conventional interstate war to provisional objectives designed to influence public opinion and leadership; and,
- Al Qaeda is not a unique or totally isolated case—hegemonic nonstate groups all over the world are threatening the stability and existence of individual nation-states and the entire world order. In this security environment, war, the power to make war, and the power to destroy or manipulate the personal security of human beings and radically change nation-states, and even the international system, is now within the reach of virtually any kind of violent nonstate actor.

In the past, the traditional security dilemma was: What is defensive, and what is aggressive? This dilemma has never really been sorted out. It depends entirely on one's interpretation on the basis of culture, values, external relationships, interests, and concepts of threat to national security. As one contemporary example, China considers the development of a large, modern navy as "defensive." Given the interests and vulnerabilities of Japan, that country considers China's efforts to be offensive—and potentially aggressive.[10] Clearly, the security dilemma of the past retains a certain validity. Nevertheless, other contemporary realities have broadened, complicated, and made more ambiguous a new (if not completely accepted) security dilemma. Accordingly, as noted above, two sets of elements are being added to the old concept: (1) hegemonic nonstate actors using unconventional methods and weapons; and, (2) political actors of all types exploiting indirect and implicit efforts to help achieve their various illicit objectives.

THE DEVELOPMENT OF THE CONTEMPORARY SECURITY DILEMMA CONCEPT

Nearly 400 years of diplomatic and military practice and international political-legal thought do not go away with a flash of realistic light. It takes years of diplomatic effort, military experience, and scholarly writing to generate significant change. There are those who find the new security dilemma concept so broad, ambiguous, and ambitious that they cannot understand how the necessary changes might be operationalized. Others are comfortable with what they have known for years and resist the required change as simply too difficult to deal with. In any event and at any point in the process of significant change, new diplomatic, military, and normative principles develop pertaining to hegemonic threats to political-economic-social stability and human well-being. These new principles, however, have been developed out of the long-existing international law of intervention for humanitarian purposes (e.g., Equity Law).[11]

Briefly examined are: (1) the relatively recent evolution of international conventions and declarations that contribute directly to the contemporary diplomatic definition of security; (2) scholarly thinking that relates directly to political-diplomatic-legal principles that have become integral parts of efforts by the United Nations and various members of the international community to confront threats to citizen and collective security and human well-being *before* they reach crisis proportions and have already caused massive human suffering; and, (3) selected post-Cold War military responses to hegemonic nonstate actors.

The security dilemma, then, is more than determining: What is aggression, and what is not aggression? It is now: Why, when, and how to intervene to protect people and prevent egregious human suffering? This dilemma, in turn, encompasses more than a redefinition of security. It is nothing less than a redefinition of sovereignty. Sovereignty was in the past the control of territory and the people in it. Sovereignty today is the responsibility to protect the well-being of people in any given territory.[12]

International Conventions and Declarations.

In 2001, Secretary General of the UN Kofi Annan followed Boutros-Boutros Ghali's 1992 analysis of the state of the world with his *Millennium Report*. In response to the *Millennium Report*, the International Commission on Intervention and State Sovereignty issued a report on August 15, 2001, entitled *The Responsibility to Protect*. This report expressed the far-reaching principle that UN member states have a responsibility to protect the lives, liberty, and basic human rights of their citizens, and that if they fail to carry out that responsibility, the international community has an obligation to step in.[13] Kofi Annan's central strategic question was: "If humanitarian intervention is, indeed, an acceptable assault on sovereignty, how should we respond to a [new] Rwanda, or to a Srebrenica?"[14]

Such interventions demand a global response and fundamental legitimization by international law. As a result, a series of conventions and declarations have been promulgated to support, clarify, and strengthen the already existing 1988 UN Convention against Illegal Drug Trafficking, the 1996 Inter-American Convention against Corruption, the UN Convention against Organized Crime, and the 2001 Organization of American States (OAS) Declaration on the Responsibility to Protect. Since then, additional conventions and declarations have been passed. They are the 2002 UN Convention against Terrorism, the 2003 Inter-American Declaration on Democracy, and the 2003 OAS Declaration on Security.[15]

The 2003 OAS Declaration on Security summarized everything the Declaration on the Responsibility to Protect required — and more. The "new" legitimatized external and internal threats to global security are outlined as follows:

- Corrupted governance;
- Extreme poverty and social exclusion;
- Terrorism, transnational crime, the global drug problem, corruption, asset laundering, and illicit trafficking in weapons;
- Trafficking in persons;
- Use of Weapons of Mass Destruction (WMD) and means of delivery;
- Attacks on cyber security; and,
- Natural and man-made disasters, other health risks, and environmental degradation.[16]

This combination of diverse threats takes us back to where we began: Two new types of threats, in addition to traditional military aggression, have been introduced into the global security arena. Security, then, becomes an all-inclusive circular process of interdependent relationships among personal and collective security of citizens, political-economic-social development, peace, democracy and effective sovereignty — and back to personal and collective security again. From this perspective, four issues must be emphasized:

1. Security is too broad and too important to pass off unilaterally to either the police or the military;

2. Effective/meaningful security, well-being, and sovereignty are broad national and transnational problems that must be addressed in a unified and legitimizing manner by all the instruments of state power (e.g., political, psychological, moral, economic, informational, and military);

3. Security in its broader context becomes a transnational problem and requires transnational solutions. Thus, security must be addressed not only by all the instruments at the disposal of a given nation-state, but also by a country's international partners and the various legitimizing international organizations; and,

4. It must be emphasized that the concept of security now includes — first and foremost — the imperative of addressing the "root causes" (e.g., poverty and inequality) of internal and external instability and violence. Otherwise, the nation-state becomes extremely vulnerable to the state-failure process.[17]

Scholarly Thinking: The Responsibility to Protect and to Prevent, and Sovereignty as Responsibility.

Humanitarian crises around the world in the post-Cold War period brought new attention to the issue of state sovereignty. Among the scholars who have examined this issue are Francis Deng and his associates at the Brookings Institution. They published a book in 1996 challenging what had been the key principle of international relations since the Treaty of Westphalia; that is, sovereign states are not to interfere in one another's internal affairs. Their book, *Sovereignty as Responsibility: Conflict Management in Africa*, argues that when nation-states do not conduct their internal affairs in ways that meet internationally accepted standards, other nations representing the international community have the right and duty to intervene to protect citizens from governments that do not fulfill their responsibilities to their peoples; that is, the "duty to protect." In essence, governments that do not protect the safety and well-being of their peoples lack legitimacy and forfeit their sovereignty.[18]

In 2004, Lee Feinstein and Ann-Marie Slaughter published an article in *Foreign Affairs* that argued that nation-states have a "duty to prevent." Thus, nations' obligations to their peoples include the commitment to refrain from acquiring and developing WMD. Additionally, Feinstein and Slaughter link the poor humanitarian conditions in failing and failed states with the challenges such governments pose to global security. They recognize the need for stronger authority for the UN, and for the redefining of the traditional (Westphalian) notion of sovereignty to reflect the responsibility to prevent governments from systematically abusing their citizens.[19]

In 2006, the learned Professor Amitai Etzioni brought Deng, Feinstein, and Slaughter together, articulating a concept of sovereignty that explicitly makes sovereignty conditional. Sovereignty is more than simple control of territory and the people in it. Sovereignty is the "duty to protect and to prevent." The implications are serious:

- First, logic and experience teach us that the maintenance of global peace and security in the 21st century requires states and international organizations to be proactive (preemptive) rather than simply reactive.
- Second, we increasingly recognize that the rules and institutions of the past are inadequate for solving a new generation of threats to the world order, e.g., failed states; regional economic crises; the spread of infectious diseases; environmental degradation; the rise of transnational criminal networks; and trafficking in arms, money, drugs, people, and human body parts.
- Third, it is not states that are in danger, but their rulers—a relatively small group of identifiable individuals who seek absolute power at home and, possibly, sponsor terrorism abroad.
- Fourth, this means that state authorities are responsible for protecting the safety, well-being, and lives of their citizens.
- Fifth, national authorities are responsible not only to their citizens, but to the international community.
- Finally, where a population is suffering serious harm as a result of internal conflict, insurgency, repression, or state failure (as only a few examples), and the state is unwilling or unable to

halt or avert a given harm, the old Westphalian principle of nonintervention must yield to the new concept of sovereignty as the responsibility to protect and prevent.[20]

Accordingly, a government that is unwilling or unable to meet its legitimizing responsibilities to protect its own people and avoid harming its neighbors cannot claim sovereignty to keep the outside world from stepping into the situation to offer protection and assistance. In justifying humanitarian intervention, Deng *et al.*, Feinstein and Slaughter, and Etzioni have turned intervention in international relations into a moral imperative. As a consequence, the new security dilemma is the question: When, where, and how to intervene for security purposes? To be practical, there is a corollary: When, where, and how to intervene in security issues to produce beneficial results? A third corollary might also be added: What new authorities do the UN and/or regional International Organizations need to enforce the new responsibility of sovereignty effectively?

This concept is not a radical or completely altruistic principle of international order. It simply extrapolates from post-Cold War developments in international relations and international law, in which old rules have proved counterproductive at best, and murderous at worst.

Some Practitioners' Views Concerning Hegemonic State and Nonstate Actors.

When a member of the UN has voluntarily signed its Charter, it is assumed that this nation-state accepts the responsibilities of membership. What do we do about nations that are not members of the UN, who would presumably be exempt from any obligations? What do we do about the 100 or more nontraditional actors involved in ongoing small, irregular, asymmetric, and revolutionary wars around the world today? In any event and in any phase of a revolutionary process, hegemonic nonstate actors have played and continue to play substantial roles in helping their own organizations and/or political patrons coerce radical political change and achieve putative power. Do these nontraditional actors require sustained national policy attention? In the opinion of some practitioners, these hegemonic players are in fact engaged in insurgency — if not war — and they shift the asymmetric global security issue from abstract to real.[21]

Ray S. Kline. In the 1970s, and as a result of the Vietnam experience, Ray Kline, a former Central Intelligence Agency (CIA) official, was among the first practitioners to recognize that contemporary war requires more than a military-industrial (economic) capability.[22] Accordingly, Kline developed a two-part formula as a systematic way to think about power, that is, $Pp = (C + E + M) \times (S + W)$. Pp = perceived power; C = critical mass (population and territory); E = economic/industrial capability; M = military capability; S = strategic purpose; and W = will to pursue national policy. Thus, Kline adds critical "mass" to "economic and military capability," and brings in "strategic purpose" and "will" to complete the equation. Interestingly and importantly, he includes $S + W$ as a multiplier. That means that a country can have all the $(C + E + M)$ in the world, but if there is no strategic purpose and will, there will be no perceived power; that is, $100 + 100 + 100 \times 0 = 0$.[23]

Kline's formula seems a lot like the basis for the Caspar Weinberger and Colin Powell Doctrines. In 1984, Secretary of Defense Weinberger outlined six conditions that a conflict should meet before the United States should consider becoming involved:

1. It should be of vital national interest to the United States and its allies;

2. Intervention must occur wholeheartedly, with a clear intention of winning;

3. There must be clearly defined political and military objectives;

4. The relationship between the objectives and the forces must be continually reassessed and adjusted if necessary;

5. There must be a reasonable assurance that the American people and Congress will support the intervention; and,

6. Commitment of U.S. military forces should be the last resort.[24]

Subsequently, General Powell, while Chairman of the U.S. Joint Chiefs of Staff, 1990-91, added another principle: Should the United States intervene in a given conflict, the operation should be short and relatively light on casualties, and clearly lead to achieving the political purpose.[25] Yet, for situations involving hegemonic nonstate actors, or even rogue states, these assumptions do not apply. They apply generally to traditional interstate military-industrial war. Later practitioners have more adequately determined the kinds and combinations of power necessary to deal with contemporary intrastate conflict.

Colonel T.X. Hammes, USMC, (Ret.). In *The Sling and the Stone*, Hammes explains that we are now involved in Fourth Generation War (4GW). He argues that,

"Just as the world has evolved from an industrial society to an information-based society, so has warfare."[26] Thus, 4GW has arrived. It does not attempt to win by defeating an enemy's military forces. Both the epic, decisive Napoleonic battle (Second Generation War), and the wide-ranging, high-tech, high-speed maneuver campaign (Third Generation War) are irrelevant. 4GW is an evolved form of insurgency rooted in the fundamental precept that superior political will, when properly employed, can defeat greater military and economic power. It uses all available networks — political, economic, social, informational, and military — to convince the enemy decisionmakers that their strategic goals are either unachievable or too costly for the perceived benefits. Using its networks, 4GW directly attacks the minds of enemy decision- and policymakers to destroy their political will.[27] Thus, the importance of the media in manipulating public opinion and of leadership in changing an opponent's position on a matter of national interest is significant.[28]

This reality releases the 4GW practitioner from the strategic necessity of defending core production assets, leaving him or her free to focus on offense rather than defense. It also relieves him or her of the logistical burden of moving vast amounts of supplies long distances. Instead, he or she has to move only ideas and money — both of which can be moved instantly.[29] This does not mean, however, that 4GW is accomplished quickly; 4GWs are lengthy. They are measured in decades rather than months or years. At the same time, the use of 4GW networks does not necessarily imply a bloodless type of war. Experience reminds us that most casualties will not be military, or caused by military weapons. Rather, most casualties will be civilian and caused by weapons for which materials are readily available in modern society (e.g., roadside mines, or Improvised Explosive Devices [IEDs]). Clearly, this fact is not helpful in generating positive public opinion, or political will. But, of course, this is exactly what the 4GW practitioner is counting on. He understands that the last man standing is the "winner."

Hammes, lastly, reminds us that 4GW is the only kind of war the United States has ever lost (e.g., Vietnam, Lebanon, and Somalia). This type of war also defeated the Soviet Union in Afghanistan and Chechnya, and France in Vietnam and Algeria. "The fact that only unconventional or 4GW has succeeded against great powers should be a key element in discussing the evolution of warfare. Unfortunately, it has been largely absent from the debate within the U.S. Department of Defense."[30]

General Rupert Smith (U.K., Ret.). General Smith is straightforward. In both the opening and closing paragraphs of The *Utility of Force: The Art of War in the Modern World,* he states:

> War no longer exists. Confrontation, conflict and combat undoubtedly exist all around the world. . . . Nonetheless, war as cognitively known to most non-combatants, war as a battle in a field between men and machinery, war as a massive deciding event in a dispute in international affairs: such war no longer exists.[31]

This is not to say, however, that armed force cannot be used effectively to achieve political-psychological purposes. One has only to see how effective a few well-disciplined soldiers, armed with simple weapons, can be, and how hard it is to defeat them and prevent them from advancing their political agenda, to realize this. Force does have utility in traditional defense, in maintaining the nontraditional security of the state and its people, and in keeping the peace on an international basis (the responsibility to protect and prevent). But, to achieve this, political and military leaders must understand exactly what they are dealing with.[32]

We must adapt our approach and organize our institutions to address the concept of unconventional intrastate war and the overwhelming reality of "War Amongst the People."[33] That is, we need a revolution in our thinking (a new paradigm, a new theory of engagement, or a new game plan). We need national and international organizations and intelligence capabilities designed to deal effectively with an enemy that has no formal army; an enemy that has no maneuver forces; an enemy that has no design for conventional battle; and an enemy that keeps each engagement particular unto itself and its setting but maintains connections through a nervous system unified by an overarching political idea.[34]

Toward a New Paradigm. General Smith postulates that "War Amongst the People" requires a paradigm of confrontation defined by the following six trends:

1. The ends for which we fight are changing from the hard objectives that decide a political outcome to those that establish conditions through which an outcome may be decided;

2. We fight among the people, not on a conventional (virtually uninhabited) battlefield;

3. Our conflicts tend to be timeless, even unending; thus, time has become an important instrument of power;

4. We fight so as to preserve the force rather than risk all to gain the military objective;

5. On each occasion, new uses are found for old weapons and organizations that are the products of past industrial wars; and,

6. The sides are mostly nonstate, comprising some form of multinational grouping against some nonstate party or parties.[35]

Lastly, it must be emphasized that this kind of war is fought against enemies who are firmly embedded in the population and cannot present a traditional strategic or operational target. No conventional act of force can ever be decisive. Winning a trial of military strength will not deliver the will of the people. Fundamentally, gaining the will of the people is the only effective objective of any use of force in modern conflict. The reality of contemporary conflict and a new paradigm is that information — not firepower — is the currency upon which war is conducted. The new instruments of power are intelligence, public diplomacy, the media, time, and flexibility. These are the basic tools of power than can ultimately capture the will of the people.[36]

Organization to Deal with a "Rhizomatic" Command System and to Generate a Total Unity of Effort. A rhizomatic command system operates with an apparently hierarchical system above ground — visible in the operational and political arenas and with another system centered in the roots underground. It is a horizontal system with many discrete groups. The system develops to suit its surroundings and purpose in a process of natural selection, and with no predetermined operational structure. Its foundation is that of the social structure of its locale. The groups vary in size, but those that survive and prosper are usually small and organized in cells whose members will not necessarily know their relationship with, or the membership of, other cells. A cell will perform a minimum of three tasks: 1) direct and sometimes lead military action;

2) collect and hold resources such as money and weapons; and, 3) direct and sometimes conduct political actions, which can range from bombing train stations, to funding schools, to electioneering. Cells will normally be allowed considerable latitude in the methods they adopt to suit the local circumstances—provided the cell is both successful and no more corrupt than what is condoned by the general movement. In all cases, the need for security is paramount.[37]

The rhizomatic command system is difficult to attack, just as rhizomatic weeds are difficult to eradicate. Rhizomes are eradicated by one of three methods: 1) digging them up; 2) poisoning or removing the nutrients from the soil; or, 3) penetrating the roots with a systemic poison. Cutting off the visible heads of rhizomes causes them to lie dormant for a time—at best. The attack on a rhizomatic command system is done best from all three directions—operations in each direction being conducted to complement the others. [38] This takes us to the need to conduct a "holistic" war with a total unity of effort.

The challenge is to come to terms with the fact that contemporary security, at whatever level, is at its base a holistic political-diplomatic, social-economic, psychological-moral, and military-police effort. The fundamental mindset must be changed from a singular military approach to a multidimensional, multiorganizational, and multinational paradigm. The main task in the search for security now and in the future is to construct national stability and citizen well-being on the same strategic pillars that supported success and effectiveness in the past.

The first pillar of success is a conceptual requirement: Develop a realistic game plan or theory of engagement to deal with hegemonic political actors, and the human and physical disasters they create.

The second pillar is an organizational requirement: The creation of planning and management structures to establish a unity of effort to plan and implement the paradigm. The third is an organizational and operational requirement. Organizationally, this pillar involves developing and implementing the appropriate combination of political, economic, informational, moral, and coercive instruments of national and international power to pursue the multidimensional requirements of the contemporary global security environment. Operationally, the pillar involves learning to understand friends as well as adversaries and assessing potential adversaries culturally, to influence their thought and behavior better. The entire effort involves training and educating leaders at all levels to carry out a 21st-century game plan against a rhizomatic enemy.[39]

The next and probably most important effort in this process is educational (cognitive). The effort is directed at civilian and military leaders to help them understand and use appropriate combinations of national and international power in institutionalizing a shift in the contemporary strategic leader development paradigm.

Combinations in Unrestricted War: A Chinese Approach to a New Paradigm. The two Chinese colonels who authored *Unrestricted Warfare*, Qiao Liang and Wang Xiangsui, are adamant. They unequivocally argue that regardless of whether a war took place 2,500 years ago or last year, the data indicate that all victories or failures display one common denominator—the winner is the national power, international power bloc, or nonstate political actor that is best organized and has implemented a combination of multidimensional efforts. [40] The French experience in Vietnam and

Algeria attests to the fact that the loser is the political actor that "ad-hoc-ed" a generally singular military effort.[41] Accordingly, the global community must come to grips with the fundamentally transformed nature of defense and security challenges in the 21st century. To do so requires a significant change in how actors are educated and organized to plan and implement contemporary war (conflict).

The purpose of combinations is to organize a system of offensive and defensive power that is a great force multiplier and facilitator within the global security arena — and would deprive the enemy of the same advantages. This system gives new and greater meaning to the idea of a nation-state or other political actor using all available instruments of power to protect, maintain, and achieve its perceived political and security interests. That is one reason Qaio and Wang call this approach "Unrestricted Warfare."[42]

The dominating characteristic of a war of this kind is political-military, economic-commercial, or cultural-moral. Within the context of combinations, there is a difference between the dominant sphere and the whole, although a dynamic relationship exists between a dominant type of general war and the supporting elements that make up the whole. As an example, military war must be strongly supported by media (propaganda/information/moral) warfare and a combination of other types that might include but are not limited to psychological war, financial war, trade war, cyber war, diplomatic war, proxy war, narco-criminal war, and guerrilla war.[43] The combination of all available ways and means of conducting conflict includes military and nonmilitary, lethal and nonlethal, and direct and indirect methods. These combinations might include but are not limited to the following:

- Conventional war/cyber war/media war (e.g., Georgia, 2008);
- Surrogate or proxy war/intelligence war/media war (e.g., Lebanon, 2006);
- Narco-criminal war/financial war/psychological war (e.g., Mexico, to date);
- Diplomatic war/media war/conventional war (e.g., Algeria, 1954-62); and,
- Guerrilla war/psychological war/narco-criminal war (e.g., Peru, to date).

Any one of the above types of or combinations can be combined with others to form completely new methods and combinations of conflict. There are no means that cannot be combined with others. The only limitation is one's imagination. As a consequence, politically effective contemporary warfare requires the services of civilian warriors—as well as professional soldiers and policemen—who can conduct persuasion-coercion-propaganda war, media war, financial war, trade war, psychological war, network (virus) war, insurgency war, chemical-biological-radiological war, etc.[44] Soldiers no longer have a monopoly on power. New civilian warriors must be included in the strategic architecture for contemporary warfare.[45]

These realities require a new cognitive paradigm that would lead strategic leaders to an understanding that, *inter alia:*
- The United States is not the only important player in the global or hemispheric security arena. For any degree of success in providing the foundations for a sustainable peace, involvement must be understood as a holistic process that relies on various national and international agencies and institutions working together in a collegial and synergistic manner.

- At the highest level, the United States and its partners in a conflict must be in general agreement with regard to the threats, end-state, and associated set of multidimensional operations to achieve their common political vision. Although such an agreement regarding a strategic or operational end-state is a necessary condition for effective partnerships, it is not sufficient.
- That agreement must be supported by an executive-level organizational structure that can identify, plan, and implement a holistic plan of action. That same structure must also ensure that all political-economic-informational-military-etc. actions at the operational and tactical levels directly contribute to the achievement of the strategic political end-state. This requirement reflects a further need to develop an end-state planning mechanism within the executive-level management structure.
- Even though the United States is not the only player in the global security arena, it can often be the most powerful and influential one. Thus, every effort must be taken to ensure partnership clarity, unity, and effectiveness by collaboratively integrating U.S. political-military planning and implementing processes with allies and partners.
- Continued and enhanced multilateral dialogues (e.g., mandatory higher education, personnel exchanges, conferences, roundtables, workshops, exercises, games, etc.) will build on mutually rewarding relationships and contribute to the strategic thought underlying multilateral security policy and strategy. Such collabora-

tion, together with a healthy exchange of ideas, is an example of the strength and potential of national and international civil-military relations.

- Information and intelligence are force multipliers, and commanders and leaders at all levels must take the responsibility for collecting and managing relevant information for their own use.
- Indirect engagement versus direct involvement is an extremely important and effective tool of statecraft in contemporary conflict situations.
- The importance of learning how to defend one's own centers of gravity as well as attacking those of an opponent—and the ultimate penalty for not doing so—cannot be overstated.
- There is value in replacing U.S. operationally oriented officers with Foreign Area Officer (FAO) diagnosticians in designing and managing indirect and direct security assistance programs.
- Contemporary conflict situations, whether they are political, commercial, or ideological/religious, are not limited; they are total. Conflict is not a kind of appendage—a lesser or limited thing—to the development or disruption of well-being. As long as destabilizers (e.g., poverty, disease, environmental degradation, etc.) exist that can lead to the destruction of a people, a society, and/or government, there will be conflict. These destabilizers are as detrimental as human determination to risk everything to take down a government violently, destroy a society, or cause great harm to a society.

Conclusions and Implications. These recommendations for beginning the processes of paradigm change — although not complete — take us beyond doing "something" for something's sake. They take us beyond developing budgets, force structure, and equipment packages for a given crisis situation. They take us beyond asking: What are we going to do? and, Who is going to command and control the effort? These imperatives take us to cooperative, collegial, holistic, and long-term planning and the accomplishment of strategic ends, ways and means that directly support the accomplishment of a 21st-century end-game.

Even though prudent governments must prepare for high-risk, low-probability conventional interstate war, there is a high probability that the President of the United States and the Congress and leaders of other powers around the world will continue to require civil-military participation in unconventional conflicts well into the future. Additionally, the spillover effects of intranational and transnational nonstate actor destabilization efforts and the resultant internal conflicts place demands on the global community — if not to solve the underlying problems or control the violence, then at least to harbor the living victims.

This does not mean that the United States must be involved all over the world all the time. It does mean, however, that the United States must rethink and renew its concept of security. In much the same way that George F. Kennan's Containment Theory of Engagement was conceived in 1947, philosophical underpinnings must be devised for a new policy to deal with more diverse threats — from unpredictable directions and by more diverse state and nonstate actors.

QUESTIONS THAT ARISE OUT OF THE CONTEMORARY SECURITY DILEMMA

General Rupert Smith postulates two sets of questions regarding the governing rules of contemporary conflict to be asked and answered in developing a new strategic-level paradigm, and in making plans to implement it. These questions are based on the notion that a strategy is composed of two fundamental elements. The first is a set of questions that deals with the context of the strategy as a whole, relating directly to the who, where, and how questions of implementing a more mature and effective security design for now and the future. The second set deals with the context of the conflict, and is, in fact, a set of recommendations for educating strategic leaders.[46] In Clausewitzian terms, all these questions are designed to help decisionmakers, policymakers, and planners understand precisely what kind of conflict they may be thinking about, what it is not, and what they must do to carry it out successfully.[47]

The First Set: The Context of a Holistic Strategy.

When we think about the possibilities of conflict, we tend to invent for ourselves a comfortable U.S.-centric vision—a situation with battlefields that are well-understood, with an enemy who looks and acts more or less as we do, and a situation in which the fighting is done by the military. We must recognize, however, that in protecting our interests and confronting and influencing a hegemonic adversary today, the situation has changed. We can see that change in several ways:

- Q1: Who is the Enemy, and what is the New Center of Gravity?
- A1a: The legal-traditional concept of threats to national security and sovereignty is based on the assumption that war is fought between geographically distinct nation-state adversaries, by means of well-equipped and easily identified military forces. Traditionally, then, the enemy was a nation-state that violated national borders and threatened the major institutions, natural resources, and external interests of another state. The primary center of gravity (the hub of all power on which all depends) was recognizable enemy military forces, coupled with the nation-state's industrial-technical capability to support military operations.
- A1b: Experience gained from hundreds of small, uncomfortable insurgency (revolutionary) wars that have taken place over the past half-century teaches us differently. At base, the enemy has now become the political actor that plans and implements the multidimensional kinds of indirect and direct, nonmilitary and military, and nonlethal and lethal, internal and external activities that threaten a given society's general well-being and exploit the root causes of internal instability. The primary and specific effort that ultimately breaks up and defeats an adversary's political-economic-social system and forces radical change is the multidimensional erosion of people's morale and political will. The better a protagonist is at conducting the persuasive-coercive effort, the more effective that protagonist will be relative to the opposition. Accordingly, as Clausewitz taught,

the contemporary primary center of gravity changes from a familiar military concept to an ambiguous and uncomfortable leadership and public opinion paradigm.[48]

- Q2: What is the Enemy's Purpose/Motive/Objective?
- A2a: One can no longer realistically expect to destroy or capture an enemy's military formation. Enemies now conceal themselves among the population in small groups and maintain no fixed address. The nontraditional, contemporary goal of becoming involved in a conflict is to establish conditions for achieving political-psychological rather than military objectives. Irregular enemies now seek to establish conditions that drain and exhaust their stronger opponents. In striving to establish these destabilizing conditions, opponents' tactical-level objectives center on attaining the widest freedom of movement and action. Operational-level objectives would include the achievement of short- and mid-term policy goals and establishing acceptance, credibility, and de facto legitimacy within the local, national, and international communities. In turn, freedom of movement and action takes us back to where we began — that is, the strategic political motive is to impose one's will on one's adversary.
- A2b: The strategic priority for some violent political actors is simply to operate a successful business enterprise. They are not intent on completely destroying the state or its institutions and replacing them with their own. Instead, they seek to "capture" the state. That is,

they want a weak entity moderately capable of functioning in the global community (banking, transportation, and providing the protection of "sovereign" status against other nation-states), but one that will allow the nonstate actor the freedom to operate with impunity and increase profits. Nevertheless, these kinds of confrontations are the organized application of coercion or threatened coercion, intended to control an opposing government and compel radical political change. To make this issue more salient, revolutionary theorist Abraham Guillen warns us that "[This is] a struggle without clemency that exacts the highest political tension."[49]

- Q3: What Interests or Security/Sovereignty Issues Does this Threaten?
- A3a: The objectives noted above represent a quintuple threat to the authority, legitimacy, and stability of targeted governments. Generally, these threats are intended to:
  — Undermine the ability of a government to perform its legitimizing functions;
  — Significantly change a government's foreign, defense, and other policies;
  — Isolate religious or racial communities from the rest of a host nation's society, and begin to replace traditional state authority with alternative (e.g., criminal or religious) governance;
  — Transform socially isolated human terrain into "virtual states" within the host state, without a centralized bureaucracy and with no official easily targeted armed forces; and,
  — Conduct low-cost actions calculated to maximize damage, minimize response, and dis-

play carefully staged media events that lead to the erosion of the legitimacy and stability of a targeted state's political-economic-social system—that is, move the state into the state-failure process.

- Q4: What is Power?
- A4a: Power is no longer simply combat firepower directed at an enemy soldier or industrial complex. Power is multilevel—a combined political, psychological, moral, informational, economic, social, military, police, and civil bureaucratic activity that can be brought to bear appropriately in the causes as well as the perpetrators of violence. It must be remembered that Germany's former Chancellor Helmut Kohl breached the Berlin Wall with the powerful Deutschmark—not aircraft, artillery, armor, or infantry. This kind of result may be achieved by those individuals familiar with Sun Tzu's "indirect approach"— brain power, an understanding of diverse cultures, an appreciation of the power of dreams, and a mental flexibility that goes well beyond traditional forms. The principal tools in this situation include: intelligence operations; public diplomacy at home and abroad; information and propaganda operations; cultural manipulation measures to influence and/or control public opinion and decisionmaking leadership; and, foreign alliances, partnerships, and traditional diplomacy.
- A4b: As a consequence, Qaio and Wang stress that warfare is no longer an exclusive "imperial garden" where professional soldiers alone can mingle. Nonprofessional warriors (hackers,

financiers, media experts, software engineers, etc.) and hegemonic nonstate organizations are posing a greater and greater threat to sovereign nations.[50]

- Q5: What is Strategic Clarity?
- A5a: Conflict now involves entire populations — large numbers of national civilian and military agencies, other national civilian organizations, international organizations, nongovernmental organizations (NGOs), and subnational indigenous actors — involved in one way or another with complex threats to security, peace, and well-being. As a result, an almost unheard of unity of effort is required to coordinate the multilateral, multidimensional, and multiorganizational paradigm necessary for successful engagement in the contemporary interdependent world.
- A5b: Former Supreme Allied Commander in Europe General John R. Galvin (U.S. Army, Retired) argues that continuous and cooperative planning among national and international civilian and military organizations, beginning with a strategic assessment of a given situation, can establish a mechanism for developing a common vision for ultimate political success (i.e., strategic clarity). After that vision is in place, shared goals and objectives, a broad understanding of what must be done or not done or changed, and a common understanding of possibilities and constraints will generate an overarching campaign plan. That plan in turn becomes the basis for developing subordinate and supporting plans that will make direct

contributions to the achievement of the desired end-state. Thus, the roles and missions of the various national and international civilian and military elements evolve deliberately — rather than in response to ad hoc "mission creep" — as the situation changes, and progress toward the achievement of a mutually agreed-upon political vision is accommodated.[51]

- Q6: What Makes Contemporary Conflict Ambiguous?
- A6a: The traditional distinction between crime; terrorism; subversion; insurgency; popular militia, mercenary, and gang activity; and warfare are blurred. Underlying the ambiguities is the fact that most of these activities tend to be intrastate affairs (i.e., not issues between sovereign states) that international law and convention is only beginning to address. Contemporary conflict is one part of several parts of one society against another. There are virtually no rules. In these wars there is normally no formal declaration of nor termination of conflict; no easily identifiable enemy military formations to attack and destroy; no specific territory to take and hold; and no single credible government or political actors with which to deal or to hold responsible. There are no legal niceties such as mutually recognized borders and Geneva Conventions to help control a situation; no guarantee that any agreement between contending parties will be honored; and no commonly accepted rules of engagement to guide the leadership of any given state or nonstate actor.

- A6b: Additionally, in this context, there is no territory that cannot be bypassed or used; no national boundaries or laws that cannot be ignored or used; no method or means that cannot be disregarded or used; no battlefield (dimension of conflict) that cannot be ignored or used; and no nation, transnational or nonstate actor or international organization that cannot be ignored or used in some combination. This is why Qiao and Wang call this kind of war/conflict 'unrestricted war.'[52]

- Q7: What Makes Contemporary Conflict Total?
- A7a: Present and future irregular asymmetric wars can be total on at least three different levels — scope, social geography, and time. In terms of scope and social geography, conflict can now involve entire populations, their neighbors, and friends. At the same time, conflict involves a large number of national and international organizations, alliances, partnerships, private voluntary organizations, NGOs, and other associated multilateral entities. As long as opposition exists capable of living among the people and risking everything to take down a government violently, destroy a society, or cause great harm to a society, there is war. This is a zero-sum game in which there is only one winner. It is therefore total.
- A7b: As a consequence, time (the long term) becomes one of the many instruments of contemporary power and statecraft. In the terms of Guillen (and other "New" and "Old" Socialist thinkers and practitioners, such as Mao Zedong) Total War (the long war) includes no

place for compromise or other options short of the ultimate political objective (radical political change). Negotiations cannot be considered a viable means to end a conflict. Rather, negotiations are tactical and operational-level means for gaining time. Vladimir Lenin was straightforward: 'Concessions are a new kind of war.'[53]

Historian J. Boyer Bell reminds us that at the beginning of the 21st century, much of the world is ripe for those who wish to change history, avenge grievances, find security in new political structures, and/or protect or reestablish old ways. Most of all, those who want to destabilize and destroy present systems to build new and supposedly better structures are not easily discouraged. They are not looking for anything tangible. They seek the realization of a dream—the Marxian rewards of history. Thus, this century, like the last, offers the prospect of war—new wars that are total and unrestricted—outside traditional rules, limitations, and conventional methods.[54]

The Second Set of Questions: The Conduct of Contemporary Conflict.

The second set of questions is designed to assist those responsible for dealing with threats imposed on the global community by hegemonic political actors. Given today's realities, the failure to prepare adequately for present and future contingencies is unconscionable. At a minimum, there are five educational and organizational imperatives needed to implement the explicit and implied tasks in the first set of questions. They are:

- Q1: What must civilian and military leaders know regarding contemporary conflict?
- A1: Civilian and military leaders at all levels must learn the fundamental nature of subversion and insurgency, with particular reference to the way in which military and nonmilitary, lethal and nonlethal, and direct and indirect force can be employed to achieve political ends, and the ways in which political-psychological considerations affect the use of force. Additionally, leaders need to understand the strategic and political-psychological implications of operational and tactical actions.

- Q2: How must civilian and military leaders conduct themselves with other professionals and civilians?
- A2: Civilian and military personnel are expected to be able to operate effectively and collegially in coalitions or multinational contingents. They must also acquire the ability to deal collegially with civilian populations and with local and global media. As a consequence, efforts that enhance interagency, as well as international, cultural awareness — such as higher education, civilian and military exchange programs, language-training programs, and combined (multinational) exercises — must be revitalized and expanded.

- Q3: What should civilian and military leaders understand about intelligence capability?
- A3: Leaders must learn that intelligence capability several steps beyond the usual is required for irregular asymmetric conflicts. This capabil-

ity involves active utilization of intelligence operations as a dominant element of both strategy and tactics. Thus, civilian leaders and military commanders at all levels must be responsible to collect and exploit timely intelligence. The lowest echelon where adequate intelligence assets have been generally concentrated is the division or brigade. Yet, such operations in most contemporary conflicts are conducted independently by battalions and smaller units.

- Q4: Should "peacekeepers" be able to do more than observe and keep belligerents apart?
- A4: Yes, certainly. Hegemonic nonstate actors in any kind of intrastate or interstate conflict are likely to have at their disposal an awesome array of conventional and unconventional weaponry. The "savage wars of peace" have and will continue to place military forces and civilian support contingents to harm's way. Thus, leadership development must prepare peace enforcers working in compliance with Chapter 6 and 7 of the UN Charter to be effective warfighters.

- Q5: What are the primary organizational requirements for dealing with contemporary conflict?
- A5: Governments must restructure themselves to the extent necessary to establish the appropriate political mechanisms for an effective unity of effort. The intent is to ensure that the application of the various civilian and military instruments of power directly contribute to a mutually agreed-upon end-state. Generating a

more complete unity of effort (strategic clarity) will require contributions at the international and multilateral levels (horizontal unity), as well as the national level (vertical unity).

As we rethink contemporary security, we must not think of ourselves as much as "war fighters" as "war preventers." Thus, it is incumbent on the United States and the rest of the global community to understand and cope with the threats imposed by contemporary nontraditional actors and think outside the box. We must replace the old Westphalian thinking with a holistic national-international and civil-military approach as it applies to the chaos (disequilibrium) provoked by the diverse state, nonstate, and transnational threats and menaces that heretofore have been ignored or wished away.

CONCLUSIONS

The above challenges and tasks are not radical. They are only the logical extensions of basic security strategy and national and international asset management. By accepting these challenges and tasks, the United States and the West (and perhaps others) can help replace conflict with cooperation, harvest hope, and fulfill the promise that a new multidimensional security paradigm offers. These cooperative efforts may not be easy to establish; however, they should prove in the mid to long term to be far less demanding and costly in political, economic, military, and ethical terms than continuing a business as usual/crisis management approach to contemporary global security.

In discussing the utopian dreams and destructive activities of hegemonic state and nonstate actors, Albert Camus admonishes us to understand that:

He who dedicates himself to the destruction of the old in order to build something new [and possibly better] dedicates himself to nothing and, in his turn, is nothing. But, he who dedicates himself to the dignity of mankind, dedicates himself to the earth and reaps from it the harvest that sows its seed and sustains the world again and again.[55]

ENDNOTES

1. Boutros-Boutros Ghali, "Global Leadership after the Cold War," *Foreign Affairs*, March/April 1996, pp. 86-98.

2. *Ibid.*, pp. 90-93.

3. See, for example, Seyom Brown, *New Forces, Old Forces, and the Future of World Politics*, New York: Harper Collins College Publishers, 1995, p. 46.

4. See: Hans J. Morgenthau, *Politics Among Nations: The Struggle for Power and Peace*, New York: McGraw Hill-Publishing Company, 1985.

5. Albert Camus, *The Rebel*, New York: Vintage Books, 1956, p. 179.

6. *Ibid.* Also see Robert Gilpin, *War and Change in World Politics*, Cambridge, UK: Cambridge University Press, 1993.

7. See, for examples, Frank N. Trager and Philip S. Kronenberg, eds., *National Security and American Society*, Lawrence, KS: University Press of Kansas, 1973; Amos A. Jordan, William J. Taylor, Jr., and Michael J. Mazarr, *American National Security*, 5th Ed., Baltimore, MD: John Hopkins University Press, 1999.

8. Kimbra L. Fishel, "Challenging the Hegemon: Al Qaeda's Elevation of Asymmetric Insurgent Warfare onto the Global Arena," in Robert J. Bunker, *Networks, Terrorism, and Global Insurgency*, London, UK: Routledge, 2005, pp. 115-128.

9. Primary source material on statements made by al Qaeda is available from *usinfo.state.gov/topical/pol/terror/99129502. html*. Also see Raymond Ibrahim, *The al Qaeda Reader*, New York: Broadway Books, 2007.

10. Edward Wong, "China's Navy Reaches Far, Unsettling the Region," *The New York Times*, June 15, 2011, p. A11.

11. Lee Feinstein and Ann-Marie Slaughter, "A Duty to Prevent," *Foreign Affairs*, January/February 2004, pp. 147-148.

12. Amitai Etzioni, "Responsibility as Sovereignty," *Orbis*, Winter 2006, pp. 1-15.

13. *Responsibility to Protect*, New York: International Commission on Intervention and State Sovereignty (ICISS), p. 13.

14. *Ibid.*, p. 2.

15. Available from *www.oas.org/document/eng/DeclarationSecurity__102803.asp*.

16. *Ibid.*

17. Max G. Manwaring, *Security in the Americas: Neither Evolution nor Devolution – Impasse*, Carlisle, PA: Strategic Studies Institute, U.S. Army War College, 2004.

18. Francis M. Deng *et al.*, *Sovereignty as Responsibility*, Washington, DC: The Brookings Institution, 1996, p. 33.

19. Feinstein and Slaughter, "A Duty to Prevent," pp. 136-150.

20. Etzioni, "Responsibility," pp. 1-15; also see *OAS Declaration on the Responsibility to Protect*, available from *www.oas.org/documents*.

21. Barry Buzan, *People, States and Fear*, 2nd Ed., Boulder, CO: Lynne Rienner Publishers, 1991; Keith Krause and Michael C. Williams, eds., *Critical Security Studies*, Minneapolis, MS: University of Minnesota Press, 1997; Mohammed Ayoob, "Defining Security: A Subaltern Realist Perspective," in Krause and Williams,

pp. 121-146; Daniel C. Esty *et al.*, "The State Failure Project: Early Warning Research for U.S. Foreign Policy Planning," in John L. Davies and Ted Robert Gurr, eds., *Preventive Measures: Building Risk Assessment and Crisis Early Warning System,* New York: Rowman & Littlefield, 1998; Anthony T. Bryan, *Transnational Organized Crime: The Caribbean Context,* Miami, FL: The Dante B. Fascell North-South Center Press, University of Miami, 2002; "El delito como una amenaza geopolitica" ("The Offence as a Geopolitical Threat"), available from *Clarin.com*, July 3, 2003.

22. Ray S. Kline, *World Power Assessment: A Calculus of Strategic Drift,* Washington, DC: Georgetown University Center for Strategic and International Studies, 1975. Others would include Wayne Ferris, *The Power Capabilities of Nation-States,* New York: D. C. Heath and Company, 1973; J. F. K. Organski and Jacek Kugler, "Davids and Goliaths: Predicting the Outcomes of International Wars," *Comparative Political Studies,* July 1978, pp. 141-181; and Colonel Harry Summers, U.S. Army (Ret.), *On Strategy: The Vietnam War in Perspective,* Carlisle, PA: Strategic Studies Institute, U.S. Army War College, 1981.

23. Kline, pp. 29-112.

24. Available from *www.mbc.edu/faculty/gbowen/weinberger. htm.*

25. Available from *en.wikipedia.org/wiki/Powell_Doctrine.*

26. T. X. Hammes, *The Sling and the Stone,* Grand Rapids, MI: Zenith Press, 2006, p. i.

27. *Ibid.,* pp. I, 210, 246-257.

28. Clausewitz and Sun Tzu warned us of all this centuries and years ago. See Carl von Clausewitz, *On War,* Michael Howard and Peter Paret, eds. and trans., Princeton, NJ: Princeton University Press, 1976; and Sun Tzu, *The Art of War,* Samuel B. Griffith, trans., Oxford, UK: Oxford University Press, 1963.

29. Hammes, p. 209.

30. *Ibid.* p. i.

31. General Rupert Smith, *The Utility of Force: The Art of War in the Modern World*, New York: Alfred A. Knopf, 2007, pp. 3, 415.

32. Clausewitz, p. 88.

33. Smith, 2007, pp. 374-385.

34. *Ibid.*, p. 331.

35. *Ibid.*, p. 271.

36. *Ibid.*, p. 334.

37. *Ibid.*, p. 332.

38. *Ibid.*, pp. 332-334.

39. John T. Fishel and Max G. Manwaring, *Uncomfortable Wars Revisited*, Norman, OK: University of Oklahoma Press, 2010, pp. 53-54.

40. Qiao Liang and Wang Xiangsui, *Unrestricted Warfare*, Beijing, China: PLA Arts and Literature Publishing House, 1999, pp. 143, 157.

41. Roger Trinquier, *Modern Warfare: A French View of Counterinsurgency*, Ft. Leavenworth, KS: Combined Arms Research Library, 1964, p. 35.

42. *Ibid.*

43. Qiap and Wang, p. 154 .

44. *Ibid.*, p. 123.

45. *Ibid.*, p. 41.

46. Smith, pp. 392, 405.

47. Clausewitz, p. 88.

48. *Ibid.*, p. 596.

49. Abraham Guillen, *Philosophy of the Urban Guerrilla: The Revolutionary Writings of Abraham Guillen*, Donald C. Hodges, ed. and trans., New York: William Morrow, 1973, pp. 278-279.

50. Qiao and Wang, p. 41.

51. Author interview with General John R. Galvin, August 6, 1997, Boston, MA. The complete interview is included in the Spring 1998 Special Issue of *Small Wars & Insurgencies*, No.1, p. 9.

52. Qiao and Wang, 1999.

53. V. I. Lenin, "Capitalist Discords and Concessions Policy," Robert C. Tucker, ed., *The Lenin Anthology*, New York: W. W. Norton & Company, Inc., 1975, pp. 628-634. Also see Guillen, 1973, p. 279.

54. J. Boyer Bell, *Dragonwars,* New Brunswick, NJ: Transaction Publishers, 1999, pp. 21-33.

55. Camus, 1956, p. 302.